Amazing Moments to Remember

Amazing Moments to Remember

BETH JOSI

RESOURCE *Publications* • Eugene, Oregon

AMAZING MOMENTS TO REMEMBER

Copyright © 2019 Beth Josi. All rights reserved. Except for brief quotations in critical publications or reviews, no part of this book may be reproduced in any manner without prior written permission from the publisher. Write: Permissions, Wipf and Stock Publishers, 199 W. 8th Ave., Suite 3, Eugene, OR 97401.

Resource Publications
An Imprint of Wipf and Stock Publishers
199 W. 8th Ave., Suite 3
Eugene, OR 97401

www.wipfandstock.com

PAPERBACK ISBN: 978-1-5326-9247-5
HARDCOVER ISBN: 978-1-5326-9248-2
EBOOK ISBN: 978-1-5326-9249-9

Manufactured in the U.S.A.   09/27/19

Contents

Introduction | vii

Chapter 1
I Remember the Moment I Became a Christian | 1

Chapter 2
I Remember the Moment When I Found God!! | 3

Chapter 3
I Remember the Moment God Gave Me a Vision to Become a Coach | 6

Chapter 4
I Remember the Moment When God Gave Me a Dream Wedding and a Trip to Europe! | 9

Chapter 5
I Remember the Moment When I Broke Away from a Religious Spirit | 15

Chapter 6
I Remember When Micki and Mitch Were Born | 17

Chapter 7
I Remember the Moments When Micki and Mitch Said Some Funny Things | 22

Chapter 8
I Remember the Moment When Micki Decided to Move to New York!! | 26

Chapter 9
I Remember the Moment When Mitch Got His First Dirt Bike | 30

Chapter 10
I Remember the Moment When God Gave Me My Dream Horse, Kipper | 35

Chapter 11
I Remember the Moment When I Met My Friend, Billy | 40

Chapter 12
I Remember the Moment When I Started a Fun Club | 47

Chapter 13
I Remember the Moment When I Became Banjo Beth | 49

Chapter 14
I Remember the Moment When God Gave Me Winnervision | 54

Chapter 15
I Remember the Moment When God Gave Me a Heavenly Attic Bed and Breakfast | 57

Chapter 16
I Remember the Moment When I Became a Housesitter | 63

Chapter 17
I Remember the Moment When I Became an Artist | 67

Chapter 18
I Remember the Moment When I Became a Single Mother | 70

Chapter 19
I Remember the Moment When I Fell Apart | 73

Chapter 20
I Remember the Moment When I Read the Story of David and Goliath | 76

Chapter 21
I Remember the Moment When I Read the Story of Joshua and Caleb | 82

In Closing | 84

Introduction

FOUR YEARS AGO I wrote five stories about my life. My friends told me how much they enjoyed them. Karen and I were having lunch, and she said, "Beth, I have enjoyed your stories so much. I think you should write more stories."

"I really cannot write anymore stories until I feel inspired by God to write them," I explained.

That conversation happened four years ago.

Good news, Karen! I have felt inspired by God to write more stories! Now, instead of five stories, I have written twenty-one stories!

These are stories about real experiences I have had, and I hope you enjoy them. I love to hear about what has happened in a person's life, and how they learned from their experiences.

This scripture is exactly what God is saying to me!

> Write the revelation and make it plain, so whoever ever reads it may run with it. (Hab 2:2)

Chapter 1

I Remember the Moment I Became a Christian

I LOVE DRAMATIC CONVERSION stories. The story of Paul being knocked off of his horse by a bright light captures my attention. God spoke to him and told him who He was. Then God blinded him, just to make sure he was listening. Next he sent someone to pray for him so he could get his sight back. Very dramatic.

Paul told his story to all the other Christians so that they knew God called Paul to serve Him. Paul had been out to put Christians in jail, and stop everyone who said they believed in Jesus. Christians lived in fear of Paul.

Suddenly, Paul was one of them, and it was very hard for them to trust him. Paul convinced them he really was a Christian like they were. Paul set out to start churches everywhere, and when he was put in prison for his faith, he wrote two thirds of the New Testament.

My conversion story was not so dramatic. It happened for me when I was five years old in kindergarten.

Even though my family was not Catholic, I was attending a Catholic kindergarten. It must have been the only one available.

I vividly remember a nun in a black habit standing in front of the class. She said, "If you want to go to heaven, ask Jesus into your heart. Ask Jesus to forgive your sins, and you will go to heaven. Jesus died for your sins."

I made a decision at five years old; I decided, yes, I want to go to heaven. I decided to pray when I got home.

I vividly remember kneeling down in front of our stuffed chair to pray. *And then it hit me.*

How could I ask God to forgive my sins? I could not think of anything I had done wrong. I needed a sin for this to work.

What could I do? And then I got an idea. Our dog, Lux, a German Shorthair Pointer, was sleeping in the living room. I got up, and hit him in the nose. He woke up and looked at me, very concerned. Then he went back to sleep.

There, done. Now I had a sin.

So I prayed that God would forgive my sin, and I asked Jesus to come into my heart. Not quite as dramatic as Paul's conversion, but I remember it vividly, like it was yesterday.

Now I was a Christian, like Paul, but I did not go to church, and I had no idea what it meant to be a Christian.

The older I got, the more I wanted a relationship with God.

When I was fifteen I started walking to a corner church, and I went forward to ask Jesus into my heart again.

I tried to read the Bible, but could not understand it. I gave up.

But God knew I was looking for Him.

He made it possible for me to find Him. This is one of my favorite scriptures:

> "Then you will call upon me and come and pray to me and I will listen to you. You will seek me and find me when you seek me with all of your heart. I will be found by you," declares the Lord. (Jer 29:12–14)

Next, I want to tell you about how I found Him.

Chapter 2

I Remember the Moment When I Found God!!

Yes !! I found God!! Where was He ? He was hiding in the Bible, but when I had tried to read the Bible, I did not understand it, so I gave up.

God knew I was looking for Him, so He sent some important people into my life.

The first person was a boy sitting next to me in history class; his name was John Franz. John was exceptionally nice, and one day he invited me to go to a Young Life meeting. I did not know what a Young Life meeting was, but I decided to go and find out.

I found out Young Life was a ministry to reach out to high school students, like me, who did not attend church.

Once I got there, the living room was filled with high school students. They sang songs, and then the leader gave a short talk about God. I enjoyed being there, so I decided to attend a Young Life Ski Camp.

The leader was there, and I started talking to him after one of the meetings. His name was Ken Doerksen. He asked me if I had read the Bible, and I told him I tried, but I had given up.

Ken gave me a copy of the Phillips translation of the New Testament.

I took it home, and starting reading it. I was amazed, because I could understand it.

I read the stories about Jesus, born in a manger, and then all about His life.

I read about how He turned water into wine, how He healed the blind, healed the deaf, walked on water, calmed the storm, took bread and two fish and multiplied it to feed thousands, healed the sick, and raised a man from the dead. I read how he was crucified, and then rose from the dead.

Not your everyday resume. I read about the promises He made to people. He offered to provide everything we need, to be with us and protect us, to lead and direct us in everything we do. He promised to give us peace and joy and to give us the desires of our hearts. He offered to keep us healthy and heal our broken hearts. He said He had a plan for our lives. He said He would forgive our sins.

I was totally in awe. Could this be true? Really?

Next I read about what Paul wrote about how to pray and follow the Lord everyday of our lives.

The more I read, the more excited I became.

I began to feel overwhelmed with God's love.

Soon, I felt a fire burning inside me that continues to burn to this day. It was a burning desire to experience more of God, and to share what I had experienced.

One day, while I was reading, I believe God spoke to me.

He said, "*I will use you to reach a generation.*"

I have told few people that He said that, because it seemed so overwhelming. I did not know how that could be possible, but I felt that God would lead me, and show me how to reach people. He gave me a purpose. I believed that He would show me what to do. I felt I had a job to do, and I wanted to do it.

Here is one of my favorite scriptures:

> Now may the God of peace equip you with all you need to do His will. May He produce in you, through the power of Jesus Christ, every good thing that is pleasing to Him (Heb 13:20–21).

Paul describes our walk with the Lord as a race. *I made a decision to step out on the track. I wanted to find out what God wanted me to do with my life.*

Here is another favorite scripture:

> All glory to God, who is able through His mighty power at work within us, to accomplish infinitely *more than we might ask or think* (Eph 3:20)

God has done more in my life than I could ask or think!

I want to share some of my experiences with you because then you will know He can lead you and help you the same way that He did for me.

When I first started reading the Bible, I felt empty and alone. My cup was empty. Once I started reading about God's love, I actually felt His love. It felt like He filled my cup to overflowing. I felt peace and joy. And now I had a purpose. He said that He would use me to reach a generation. . . ..how could that be possible? All I knew is that I wanted to try.

> For my thoughts are not your thoughts, neither are your ways my ways, declares the Lord, as the heavens are higher than the earth, so are my ways higher than your ways, and my thoughts higher than your thoughts. (Isa 55:8)

> I can do all things through Christ who strengthens me. (Phil 4:13)

Chapter 3

I Remember the Moment God Gave Me a Vision to Become a Coach

I WAS AT A loss because I had left college to take care of my mother who passed away from cancer.

My father had remarried, and I was free to go back to college, but I did not have a major.

I prayed non-stop, and asked God what to do.

Then God did a miracle.

I was working at the YMCA teaching tennis and swimming to children. One day my boss, Mr. Todd, walked to the pool and asked me to go to lunch so he could talk to me.

I had no idea what he wanted to talk to me about.

We drove one mile down the road to the A&W root beer stand and sat in the car.

"I want to talk to you about going back to college to major in Physical Education. I have been watching you teach and *you have a gift for teaching*," he said.

My reaction was very negative.

"I would have to take Anatomy, Physiology, and Kinesiology all in one year. I don't think I could pass those classes. Besides, it is such a negative field. *I don't think I can do it,*" I said.

"You could make a positive difference. If you decided to do it, I believe you could pass those classes," he said.

I Remember the Moment God Gave Me a Vision to Become a Coach

I was not convinced. We drove back to the Y in silence.

Two weeks later, Mr. Todd came to the pool again and asked me to go to lunch again.

We drove back to the A&W root beer stand, and sat in the car again. He said exactly what he had said the first time!!

All of a sudden, when he was talking, *God gave me a vision! I saw myself standing on a tennis court, teaching tennis!*

"Mr. Todd, I think you are right. I think I will go back to college, and major in Physical Education."

I went back to college and majored in Physical Education. I prayed my way through school. I asked for God's help so I could pass the classes I needed to pass. In the Bible it says, if you need wisdom, then ask for it. I prayed for supernatural wisdom. What seemed impossible to me, God made possible! Once I graduated, *I saw my vision become reality.*

How did my vision become reality?

Several years after I graduated, I was hired at the University of California at San Diego to be a Recreational Director, and the Women's tennis coach.

I remember standing on the tennis courts thinking, *"This is exactly what I saw in my vision! This is happening, this is reality!"*

Today I marvel at what happened. I prayed for help to know what to do, then Mr. Todd talked to me about majoring in Physical Education.

I believe God helped me to pass the classes I needed to pass.

The miracle to me is not just that Mr. Todd took the time to talk to me, but *that he talked to me twice!!*

I marvel that God gave me a vision!

Mr. Todd was the only person who ever told me that *I had a gift for teaching.* He is the only person who ever told me that *I could make a positive difference.*

I don't know what I would have done if Mr. Todd had not talked to me. I don't know if I would have gone back to college or not. God used Mr. Todd to change my life.

I left the Y to go back to school, and Mr. Todd left to work at another Y. I never had a chance to thank him for talking to me.

This is such a dramatic example of how God answered my prayers, and led me in the direction that He wanted me to go. This is why I always ask God for direction for my life!

Here are some of my favorite scriptures:

> Without a vision, the people will perish. (Prov 29:18)

> If any of you lacks wisdom, he should ask God, who gives generously to all without finding fault, and it will be given to him. (Jas 1:5)

> And we know that in all things God works for the good of those who love Him, who have been called according to his purpose. (Rom 8:28)

All the way through school I thought about the vision God had given me.

The good news is that the *vision became reality*!

Chapter 4

I Remember the Moment When God Gave Me a Dream Wedding and a Trip to Europe!

I prayed all of my life that I could get married someday, go to Europe someday, and have a family someday.

God answered all my prayers!

My husband Roy and I met at Oregon State at a Campus Crusade for Christ meeting. His name was Roy Josi.

He graduated from a ROTC program, and then left to go into the Navy. He was on a destroyer that went out to sea for weeks and months at a time.

We had a dream wedding in Oregon, and then we left for Norfolk, Virginia so we would live close to the ship.

Why do I say it was a dream wedding? I was able to marry the man I wanted to marry; my father walked me down the aisle; I found the perfect dress; Linaya was one of my best friends, and my maid of honor. We got married in the most beautiful church I have ever seen to this day. I have included pictures of me, my Dad, my Dad walking me down the aisle, Linaya and me, Roy and I cutting the cake!

Once we got to Norfolk I met the other officers' wives. They told me they were all planning to go to Europe because the ship was going to Europe and would be gone for six months. They all encouraged me to go. I had always had a dream to go to Europe, but I did not know how it could ever happen.

I decided I would go with them. I got a job and earned the money to buy a ticket on an ocean liner to get there, and a Eurail pass to travel on the train once I got there.

I bought a book that said *Europe on Five Dollars a Day*. It had the locations of all the youth hostels in Europe.

After I bought my ticket, I found out that all the other wives decided to stay home. It meant I would be traveling in Europe alone!

When I was on the ship, I met a young couple and their son, Leo. They were going back to Portugal to visit their family. Their family lived in a tiny village 100 miles north of Lisbon.

We became friends, and they invited me to go to their tiny village so I could see Portugal. I decided to get off the ship early and go with them.

When I got off the ship, *I went into culture shock!* We got in a large taxi and started the trip to the little village.

When I looked out the window, I saw women walking along the road with huge baskets on their heads. I was amazed!

It took hours to get there, and everything became more remote!

Once we got there, I got a tour of the village. About 100 people lived there. They all lived in small huts.

When it was time for dinner, they went out and killed a rabbit, and picked some lettuce out of the garden ! Again, I was amazed!

There was no indoor plumbing or even an outhouse. To go to the bathroom, you just went out to the barn. You looked for a pile of hay!

There was a donkey there that was rideable. I got to ride the donkey through the fig orchards! That is a favorite memory!

There was a community bath house with one bath tub. No, I did not take a bath in it !

There were no cars, just the one taxi that came and went once in awhile. I took the taxi back to Lisbon, and then took a train to meet Roy in Spain when his ship came in.

He had five days off, so we decided to go to Aldelboden, Switzerland, to see if we could meet some of his relatives. Roy's sister said there were relatives that lived there. At least their last name was Josi.

The only way to get there was on a bus. Once we got there, we found out there was no way to leave, so we went to the tourist office to see if we could find a place to stay.

We asked if there were some people in the village by the name of Josi. The lady at the desk made a call.

Soon, a man about 75 years old, walked into the tourist office. His name was Johan Josi. He was a saddle maker. He did not speak English, but he told the tourist lady he would take us to his house to meet his children who spoke English.

His children came over, and Roy showed them his ID. Roy told them he thought we were their relatives.

They were very nice, and said we could stay in their guest room. It was usually rented out to skiers, but it had not snowed there yet that year.

That night it snowed three feet! We went skiing the next day!

We walked through the village, and went into the local church. On the wall was the Josi family crest. That meant they had helped start the church. Standing there looking at the family crest was an amazing moment!

Since we were in Switzerland, we decided to visit the famous mountain, the Matterhorn. There is a small village at the base of the mountain called Zermatt. I remember sitting in a little restaurant in Zermatt eating cheese fondue for the first time. Another favorite memory!

We took the train back to Spain, and Roy got back on the ship.

I was on my way back to the youth hostel when my purse was stolen!

I lost my Eurail pass, and my money!

God did a miracle!

As soon as the youth in the hostel heard about it, they did something amazing. Even though they barely knew me, they took up an offering, and gave me some money! Not only that, they offered to let me travel with them! They traveled by hitch-hiking! I experienced hitch-hiking for the first time, *fun!*

One of my favorite places to visit was Salzburg, Austria. I got to go to the house where they filmed The Sound of Music! I got to walk around in the back yard and see the back patio and walk down to the river. The Sound of Music was my favorite movie, so it was a dream come true for me to actually be at the house where it was filmed. A moment to remember!

Another favorite experience was standing in the Sistine Chapel looking up at the painting on the ceiling! A moment to remember, very overwhelming. I loved seeing the statue of David, too. So amazing to see it in person!

After six months, I flew home and met Roy when the ship came in. Then we found out he would be leaving for a year. His ship would be off the coast of Japan. Roy decided I should move to San Diego so he could get stationed there when he got back.

Instead of flying to San Diego, we decided to camp across country. We were driving a little VW bug, and our dog, Tyke, rode in the back seat. That trip took my desire to camp away for years!

Once we got to San Diego, I got a job at the YWCA as a Recreation Director. I taught swimming, tennis, and set up summer camps for children.

I left that job, and was hired as the Recreation Director and Women's Tennis Coach at the University of California at San Diego.

When I was standing on the tennis courts, I thought about the vision God had given me! *Now the vision was reality!*

After coaching for two years at UCSD, we moved back to Oregon, and I coached for two years at Estacada High School.

I Remember the Moment When God Gave Me a Dream Wedding and a Trip to Europe!

Amazing Moments to Remember

Chapter 5

I Remember the Moment When I Broke Away from a Religious Spirit

When Roy and I met we were involved in Campus Crusade for Christ. We both felt pressure to talk to everyone about becoming a Christian. During the year Roy was gone, I burned out from the pressure to talk to everyone about becoming a Christian. I did not want to feel the pressure anymore. I made a decision to break away from the pressure. *I felt it was a religious spirit, and I resented it.*

I went from one extreme to the other. I stopped going to church. I stopped reading the Bible. I stopped praying or talking to God. I avoided being around any Christians. My attitude was, "Don't talk to me about God."

I lived that way for years. *I saw the worst in myself because I did not have a close relationship with the Lord anymore.*

Then one day, it hit me. The way I was living was very wrong. I decided to talk to God again.

"Lord, it is me. I don't know what to do. I cannot go back to living a religious life. I felt too much pressure. It robbed me of any joy that I used to feel," I said.

I felt He heard me, and He said, *"Do not go back. Go forward. Relax. Enjoy a relationship with me again. I did not put the pressure on you. Satan put pressure on you to steal your joy."*

And then I said, "*But I have been so wrong. Can you forgive me?*"

I actually felt God's forgiveness. I felt he understood why I rebelled against the religious spirit. I needed to forgive myself for wasting years of my life living without a relationship with God.

These are the scriptures that helped me to feel forgiven and to be able to have a relationship with God again.

> The thief comes only to steal and kill and destroy; I have come that they may have life, and have it to the full. (John 10:10)

> I will restore you to health and heal your wounds. (Jer 30:17)

> Come now, let us reason together says the Lord. Though your sins are like scarlet, they shall be as white as snow; though they are red as crimson, they shall be like wool. (Isa 1:18)

> Forget the former things: do not dwell on the past. (Isa 43:18)

> One thing I do: forgetting what is behind and straining toward what is ahead, I press on toward the goal to win the prize for which God has called me heavenward in Christ Jesus. (Phil 3:13)

> Therefore, if anyone is in Christ, he is a new creation, the old is gone, all things become new. (2 Cor 5:17)

Every day I thank God for helping me to put the past in the past so I can live in present time.

Chapter 6

I Remember When Micki and Mitch Were Born

I PRAYED ALL OF my life that I could have a family someday.

Micki and Mitch have been the best gift God has ever given me!

I loved watching them grow up.

To be a good mother, I knew I needed God's help. My mother was not a happy person. She was depressed during the day, and started drinking at night.

I could never talk to her about anything. She did not ever compliment me; she only criticized me. Because she criticized me, I also criticized myself. I did not know how to feel good about myself. She never told me that she loved me; she never told me that she was proud of me. She did not make me feel loved.

I wanted a happy, healthy mother, but I did not have one. I tried to talk to her about the Lord, but she was not interested.

I thought maybe I could change her. I stopped trying in school to get her attention. I brought home straight D's. I thought I could tell her I needed her to stop drinking.

It did not work. She yelled and screamed at me until she lost her voice.

I went to my room and made a decision. I would not try to change her anymore. I realized I needed to stop thinking about her, and try to help myself the best I could. She was an example of the mother I did not want to be. I prayed that God would help me learn how to feel good about myself.

I needed help so I did not become a depressed person. I needed to learn how to stop criticizing myself and stop putting myself down.

She never changed. I left college to take care of her when she passed away from cancer. I was twenty at the time.

Just before she died, I asked her if she would like to become a Christian so she could go to heaven. She said yes, so I prayed with her. I am hoping that I will see her in heaven. I was able to forgive her, because I knew if she had experienced the Lord in her life she would have been a healthy, happy person.

The good news is that I felt loved by my father. He was an extremely positive person. I cannot remember him ever saying one negative thing to me or about anyone. He not only told me that he loved me, but I could actually see love pouring out of his eyes.

I got to go hunting with him; and he taught me to play golf. I had fun with him; and I felt like I could talk to him. He even explained the game of football to me! *He was everything I could have wanted as a father!*

One day he told me he was planning on providing me with a college education. What a gift.

I also felt blessed to have my older brother, Rusty. I felt that he actually cared about me. He was five years older, and he became my role model. He was active in school, played three sports, and was very outgoing. He is, to this day, probably the most driven person I have ever met.

One day he came into my room and said, "Do you have any goals? Do not be a person who sits around and does nothing. Do not wait around for other people. Stay active and live your own life."

I have never forgotten his advice. He lived the Nike commercial before it ever existed: *Just Do It*. I decided to try to live it the way that he did.

Another day he came into my room and said, "If you tell someone you are going to do something, then do it." I try to live that way every day, too.

Although I did not have the relationship with my mother that I wanted, my relationship with both my father and with Rusty gave me confidence.

I also enjoyed having a close relationship with Rusty's sons, Doug and Mike. I got to watch them grow up before Micki and Mitch were born.

My brother was a positive role model, and so were my cousins. They were all successful in school and in sports. They were all out-going and positive. I especially enjoyed a close relationship with both Jimmy and Sue who were just one year older than I was.

I also felt loved by two friends I met at an early age. Margie, I met at thirteen, and Linaya I met at eighteen. We are still close friends to this day!

Both Margie and Linaya became like sisters to me. They were both there for me when I went through the hardest times in my life. The three of us have tried to get together to celebrate our friendship through the years even though we live miles apart. I talk to Linaya every night on the phone, and Margie several times a week. Their friendship helps me feel loved every day.

God has blessed me with other close friends, too. When I was twenty- five years old, I met Kate, and then I met Mary. We live miles apart, but still stay in touch. When I was pregnant with Micki, I met Jannette, who lived across the street. She became a second mother to Micki. Twenty years ago I met Bevra, Kelly and Kevin. In the last ten years I have met Dorena, Deanne, Karen and Tracy. They are all very important in my life!

The good news is that I finally learned to stop putting myself down.

One day, God spoke to me, and he changed my life.

He said, "*Stop putting yourself down.* When you put yourself down, you are playing into Satan's plan for your life. He wants to defeat you, and keep you from being successful. *The truth is that you have unlimited potential.* From now on, instead of putting yourself down, say, '*I have unlimited potential.*' *This will set you free to be all you can be.* Take the limitations off of yourself, and off of me."

"*Wow!*" I said. *I stopped putting myself down!* What a relief to finally feel free of all the negative criticism that I had imposed on myself for so many years!! *Finally, I could feel good about myself!!*

God spoke to me over forty years ago, and every day I say to myself, "*I have unlimited potential. God loves me and he has a plan for my life. He will use me to reach other people.*"

It set me free to be a happy, healthy mother for Micki and Mitch. I was able to put them first in my life. I was able to share everything that I loved to do with them. I was able to share the Lord with them. I remember when they both became Christians.

I prayed with Micki to become a Christian when she was three years old. Mitch became a Christian when he was eight years old. One day he said to me, "I need you to pray with me! I want to be a Christian like A. C. Green." A. C. Green is his favorite professional basketball player

I will never forget one day when my daughter, Micki, said: "I could not have any higher self-esteem." It was a rewarding moment for me. My goal was to help both Micki and Mitch feel good about themselves, and to know that God has a plan for their lives.

What I wanted most in life is to give them a happy, healthy mother that they could talk to and know I would be there for them, no matter what. I wanted them to see me happy and not depressed. I wanted them to see me having a close relationship with God.

I have included some pictures for you.

The first picture is one of Rusty, Mike, Doug, Mitch and Roy. The second picture is of Micki, Mitch and me. The third picture is of me, Linaya, and Margie. Linaya is standing above me, Margie below me.

I Remember When Micki and Mitch Were Born

Chapter 7

I Remember the Moments When Micki and Mitch Said Some Funny Things

My daughter, Micki, said some funny things that I can never forget!

I picked her up from kindergarten and when we were driving home, she said, " I want to go to a Christian kindergarten. I miss the singing."

"I don't know of a Christian kindergarten," I said.

"Well . . . *look into it*," she said. "Yes, I found one!"

This has become a classic statement we seem to use a lot!

Another time when we were driving, she said, "I know what I am going to be when I grow up. I will be president of the United States, an astronaut or . . . a babysitter." She was five at the time.

One time when she was five, we were riding the train for fun to go to Eugene. Sitting across the aisle a few rows down, was an older man dressed in a business suit. Suddenly she got out of her seat, and decided to introduce herself to him.

"Hi. My name is Micki, what is your name? " she asked.

"My name is Gray," he answered.

"Well, Gray, do you know Jesus?"

"No," he replied.

"*Well, I know him, and I know where he lives!*"

Then she came back to her seat.

I Remember the Moments When Micki and Mitch Said Some Funny Things

Another day, when Micki was five, I took her to visit Roy at work. We walked into his office at PGE. It was very quiet there.

Micki did not seem impressed with his office. Then she said, "*Take me to see the big boss! I want to meet the big, big boss!*"

One day it was very quiet in Micki's room where Micki and Mitch were playing.

I walked into Micki's room. I saw Mitch sitting on the floor; Micki was standing behind him. She had just emptied an entire container of baby powder on his head! Mitch looked like he had Mt. Hood sitting on top of his head!

This time Micki did not say anything, but she was smiling, like she had just done a great job of covering him with the baby powder. I did not know what to say either; I just ran and got my camera! What a great picture!

Micki and Mitch had a great pony to ride, Donovan. Micki was playing in the house wearing her tutu. I wanted to take her picture on Donovan.

"Today is picture day; I need you to change your clothes," I said.

"I don't want to change my clothes," she replied.

"Ok, then you can wear your tutu," I said.

I got one of my favorite pictures of her on Donovan wearing her tutu and a cowboy hat!

When she was twelve, I took Micki to the abby for a cultural outing.

We were walking through the halls, and it was very quiet. There were no nuns in sight at the time. All of sudden, in a very loud voice, she said, "*Is everyone here a virgin?*"

I was happy we were all alone at that moment!

My son, Mitch, said some funny things, too.

When he was seven, he told me he was ready to play football. He wanted to try out for a team. I had to tell him that he was too young to play, he could not try out for a team. Then he said, "That means my life is over. If I can't play football, then who am I?" A very dramatic moment.

One day I walked into his room, and it was all closed up on a hot day.

"It is hot outside, why don't you open the windows?" I asked.

"*I want it to smell like a football locker room,*" he answered.

Another day I walked into his room and he had put all his GI Joes in a circle.

"Why are the GI Joes in a circle?" I asked.

"*They are having a Bible study,*" he explained.

One day he announced he was going to jump his bike off the front porch.

"I think I can do it," he said.

"I don't think it will work," I replied.

"I will show you that I can do it," he insisted.

I was hoping he was right, and that I was wrong.

He took his bike to the end of the porch, rode it as fast as he could, jumped off the front porch, and landed in a heap. He split his chin open.

I was so glad Roy was home; he took him to the ER for stitches.

As soon as he got home, he said, "*Now I know what I did wrong . . . watch this.*"

There was no point in trying to talk him out of it. He had a vision! Yes, this time it worked! He did it!

I laugh every time I think of these stories!

I have included some pictures of Micki and Mitch when they were the ages of these stories!

The last picture is the picture of Micki sitting on Donovan in her tutu!

I Remember the Moments When Micki and Mitch Said Some Funny Things

Chapter 8

I Remember the Moment When Micki Decided to Move to New York!!

MICKI GRADUATED FROM THE University of Oregon, and then she got a job working for a Credit Union in Eugene, Oregon.

The Credit Union sent her to New York City for a training session. The people there were impressed with her. They asked her to move to New York City to work for them, and they even offered to pay her way there!

It sounded like an exciting opportunity. I remember the moment when she decided to move to New York for the adventure of living in New York City. "If I don't like it, I can always move back," she said.

She left with one suitcase, found the cheapest apartment she could find, and went to work at the Credit Union in New York City.

Little did we know she would live in New York for twelve years!

After working at the Credit Union for a while, *she heard of an amazing opportunity that sparked her interest.*

There was a program being offered for professional people who lived in New York who might want to become math or science teachers, *The Fellow's Program.*

I Remember the Moment When Micki Decided to Move to New York!!

New York City had a shortage of math and science teachers. The program was designed to draw professional people into the classroom.

The program offered to pay for a master's degree in Education if they would agree to teach.

The requirement was to take a state test in math to qualify.

I was visiting Micki in New York and so I went with her to hear all about the program. I remember sitting in the room filled with professional people.

Both Micki and I felt this program was a perfect opportunity for her to become a teacher. She developed an interest in teaching math when she was in the eighth grade.

When Micki was in the seventh grade, the math teacher told her he did not think she could handle taking an advanced math class.

She talked to him and told him she wanted to try to take the class, so he let her in to see if she could do it.

She got the highest grade in the class in the seventh grade, the eighth grade, the ninth grade, and all the way through high school!

Micki decided to take the state math test to see if she could qualify for *The Fellow's Program. She passed the test, and so she was hired.*

She started teaching without any training. She taught all day, and then went to school at night to get her master's degree in Education.

She taught 6th, 7th, 8th, and 9th grades. She set a goal to save enough money to move home and buy a car and a house. It took twelve years, but she saved $60,000!!

She wanted to move home, but she felt she needed to get a job before she moved. A friend told her about a job opening at Portland Community College.

She got an interview, and flew to Oregon to apply. They asked her to teach for ten minutes for a group of math teachers. After she taught for ten minutes, they asked her if she had any questions.

"When will I know if I have the job?" she asked.

"You have the job," they replied.

She was hired on the spot! Very unusual!

Once she got home, she bought her dream car. Then she started looking on line to start dating.

She met her husband, Kristian. He had been living in Hawaii when she was living in New York. They both moved to southeast Portland within ten minutes of each other!

Now they have their dream house, and Micki has the garden she has always wanted. A huge change from cement and subways!

I do have some vivid memories when I went to visit her in New York. We were sitting in a restaurant called the Windows of the World. It was on the 110th floor of the World Trade Center. We have a picture sitting by the window toasting the Statue of Liberty which we could see from there.

"Planes fly this high," I said.

Two weeks later was 9/11, and the Trade Center was gone! We could have been there when it happened!

Another vivid memory was going to a Broadway play. It was so fun to be there in person after hearing about Broadway all my life.

Today I enjoy helping her fix up her dream house, and her dream garden!

I marvel at how God helped her find her calling as a math teacher. If she had not been living in New York she could have never become a part of *The Fellow's Program*. She loves teaching math, and is a very gifted teacher. She also loves doing Yoga, and has recently become a Yoga instructor.

Last night Micki called and read me two notes from students thanking her for helping them to overcome their fear of math. They both became A students in math for the first time in their lives!

Micki and Kristian are looking into adopting children because Micki has had some health issues.

Every day I thank God for Micki. She is everything I could have ever hoped for in a daughter. I feel so fortunate that instead of living in New York, she only lives an hour away!

I have included a picture of Micki and Kristian!

I Remember the Moment When Micki Decided to Move to New York!!

Chapter 9

I Remember the Moment When Mitch Got His First Dirt Bike

For some reason, Mitch started asking for a dirt bike as soon as he could talk. He was seven when he got his first dirt bike, and he has loved riding dirt bikes ever since.

We had an open field in front of our house, and Mitch built a jump the first day he got his bike!

A friend of mine, Ranee, has a son named Isaiah. Isaiah was begging for a dirt bike, but Ranee told me she did not know how to buy one, and did not have the money to buy one.

Mitch decided to find a dirt bike for him, and he bought it so she could make payments for it. It looked just like Mitch's bike, but the smallest size.

Isaiah turned nine years old, and he got the new dirt bike for his birthday. To this day it is the best birthday he has ever had. He jumped on, and rode like a pro! Mitch became his idol. It was fun for me to go out on day trip with them and see them ride together!!

Sometimes I would take Mitch out to my friend's property to ride his dirt bike, and I would ride my horse, Kipper.

Mitch was always looking for a place to jump his bike. One day he saw a hill in front of him, and he decided to get as much air as he could. He jumped in the air, and then landed in a huge pool of water! Roy happened to be there, and was able to help pull him and the bike out of the water!

Mitch met a friend who had a cabin at the beach. They both bought four wheelers with special tires to ride over the dunes. They had fun taking pictures of each other jumping to see who could get the most air.

Mitch is very athletic, and it was fun for me to teach him to play golf. I rented a golf cart, and of course he found a way to jump it to get some air! It was a fun ride! We could only do that when we were out of sight of the club house!

The very first day I taught him to ski we went to the top of the hill, and I showed him how to turn and how to stop. It was easy for him to ski because he was already an excellent ice skater. His legs and ankles were strong from ice skating.

"So this is how you turn, and this is how you stop, " I explained.

"Ok, got it. I will see you at the bottom of the hill." And then he took off!

I found him at the bottom of the hill.

"If you ski over there to the right side of the hill, there is a place you can jump and get a lot of air," he explained.

Nice to know, but I did not do any jumping! He did that on his very first run down the hill!

I enjoyed taking Mitch with me to my *Winnervision* seminars to teach high school athletes to stay focused under pressure. I took him with me when the first basketball team I worked with won the state championship.

He was nine years old, and playing on a basketball team.

"I need you to talk to my basketball team," he said.

"Ok, I will do it," I replied.

I was shocked to see the response of the nine-year-olds!! I was used to working with high school students. The nine-year-olds learned to stay focused faster than the high school students!

It was also fun to watch Mitch play. He was high point man two years in a row!

Even though Mitch loved to ride his dirt bike, he was an excellent horseback rider.

One day we watched the movie, The Black Stallion.

"I want a big black horse," he said.

I decided to talk to my neighbor who had a black horse out in his field. The horse was about 100 pounds under weight; you could actually see his ribs. His coat was more brown than black because he was under nourished.

He agreed to let me lease the horse in trade for caring for him at my house.

Mitch and I wormed him, and then we took him out to my friend's pasture. My horse, Kipper, was already out there in the pasture all by himself.

They became fast friends, and they took off running across the field together!

Mitch and I saw an amazing transformation.

Weeks later, this undernourished horse gained 100 pounds! His coat became a silky black, and he was absolutely beautiful!

Of course, Mitch named him "Black" after the black stallion.

I marveled when I watched Mitch get on Black. Mitch was only nine years old, and Black was a tall horse. Mitch never asked me to lift him into the saddle. Somehow he just pulled himself all the way up into the saddle. I was amazed every time he got on!

When I went out to ride Kipper, if I did not have a rider for Black, it did not matter! Black would run alongside of us just like he had a rider!

When I brought the horses back home, I saw the neighbor driving down the driveway towards the house. I was nervous he would tell me he wanted Black back because he had become so beautiful.

"I have noticed how you have taken care of my horse," he said.

"Oh, no," I thought to myself, "Now he is going to ask me if he can have Black back."

I was shocked and relieved when that is not what he said!

"*You have done such a good job taking care of him, I would like to give him to you and your son,*" he said.

Black was a perfect second horse, and a wonderful gift!

Here are a few scriptures that I love to think about.

I Remember the Moment When Mitch Got His First Dirt Bike

Those who hope in the Lord will renew their strength. They will soar on wings like eagles; they will run and not grow weary, they will walk and not faint. (Isa 40:31)

I have come so that they may have life, and have it to the full. (John 10:10)

I will guide you in the way of wisdom and lead you along straight paths. When you walk, your steps will not be hampered; when you run, you will not stumble. (Prov 4:11, 12)

This is the day the Lord has made; let us rejoice and be glad in it. (Ps 118:24)

I am with you and will watch over you wherever you go. (Gen 28:15)

Every day I thank God for being with me, and answering my prayers!

Micki is everything I could have ever asked for in a daughter, and Mitch is everything I could have ever asked for in a son!

Every time I am with them . . . I am having fun!

I have included some pictures of Mitch on his dirt bikes!

Amazing Moments to Remember

Chapter 10

I Remember the Moment When God Gave Me My Dream Horse, Kipper

My story about Kipper really starts when I was ten years old. My mother would drop me off at the movies every Saturday, and I watched Roy Rogers movies. It cost ten cents to get in.

I vividly remember, to this day, watching Roy Rogers galloping down dirt roads on his horse, Trigger. An excellent rider, he looked like he was having the time of his life! My dream to have a horse and ride like Roy Rogers was born!

I asked my father if I could have a horse; he told me we could not afford it. We did not live in the country, and we had no place to keep a horse.

Someday... someday... I believed I would have a horse and ride like Roy Rogers.

That day finally came!

I started by riding a small paint horse, but after I rode him for a while, I wanted a bigger stronger horse so I could run him and not worry about him.

I sold my first horse, and then decided to look for a horse to buy even though I did not have the money I needed at the time.

A new ranch opened about five miles from where we lived. I drove over there, and spotted Kipper. He was the biggest horse in the herd, and the leader of the pack.

I got on to ride him around the ranch. A young cowboy rode up to me and said, "I have the fastest horse on the ranch."

It made me curious. I wanted to know how fast his horse was.

"Do you want to race?" I asked.

"Sure!" he answered.

We lined up side by side. We could see the top of a hill about a quarter mile ahead so we had a finish line.

"*Get set, go!*" I said, and we were off!

At first we rode side by side. The hoofbeats were pounding the ground so loud, I can still hear the sound!

I decided to lean forward to see if my horse had another gear ... *All of a sudden my horse bolted ahead of the other horse, and we left them in the dust!*

When we got to the top of the hill, the cowboy said, "That is one fast horse you have there!"

I was overwhelmed!! I had never gone that fast on a horse, and I knew I wanted to buy him!! The problem was I did not have the money I needed.

When I got back to the barn, I told the ranch owner that I wanted to buy him.

"I will give you all the money I have!" I said.

"How much is that?" he asked.

"Ten dollars, but I could make payments," I answered.

"Sounds good to me," he agreed, and set up a payment plan for me.

I named him Kipper, and I now had the dream horse I had always wanted! He was only seven, so he was strong and fast, and he loved to run as much as I did !!

I was living in San Diego at the time, and there were dirt roads all through the hills. I loved to open him up and gallop down the dirt roads just like Roy Rogers!

I usually rode alone, but I had a border collie, Tyke, and he could run as fast as Kipper did!

Roy decided to get a horse, too, and we took the horses camping in the mountains. It was the most fun I had ever had in my life! I loved riding all day, then I loved sitting around the bonfire at night.

I Remember the Moment When God Gave Me My Dream Horse, Kipper

I have to tell you a funny story that happened when Roy and I decided to take a long ride and camp out under the stars in a remote place. We decided to rough it, so we took some dehydrated food to cook over a campfire. This was going to be high adventure. We did not have a map. We decided to follow the trail until we got tired, then make camp just like the cowboys did.

We rode and rode and rode, and we were starting to get tired. Maybe it was time to make camp and cook our dehydrated food. We looked around for some pasture for the horses.

All of a sudden, we heard something not far up the trail. It sounded like people talking. We rode a little while, and rode right into a set of corrals set up for horses that were a part of a rental string!

A cowboy walked up to us and asked, "Can I help you?"

"Where are we?" I asked.

"You are at a resort. There is a restaurant just down the trail. These corrals are for our rental horses. We take people out on rides."

"Oh, can we go to the restaurant? Can we put our horses in the corrals, and camp nearby?" I asked.

"Sure!" he said.

So much for dehydrated food and "roughing it"!!

We walked down the trail to the restaurant, and had the best steak dinner we had ever had!! Such a great memory of our trip to experience "roughing it"!!

Yes, I loved to run on Kipper, but I did not always run. I loved walking along trails with wild flowers on both sides of the trail, and climbing mountains to see the view from the top.

Kipper was so strong he loved to climb mountains, and when we got to the top, he would let out a big sigh like he was proud of himself for getting me there. He looked around like he enjoyed the view as much as I did.

I feel the closest to God when I am out riding in the woods. I feel so much peace. A peace that passes all understanding. A peace you cannot put into words, or describe to anyone. I marvel over

God's creation. How could he make all the earth so beautiful? I try to soak in all the beauty around me.

I had Kipper 25 years. I have owned other horses after Kipper, but he was the best horse I have ever had. He was my dream horse that became reality.

Some of my favorite scriptures are:

> Take delight in the Lord, and He will give you your heart's desires. (Ps 37:4)

> Now may the Lord of peace himself give you peace at all times and in every way. (2 Thess 3:16)

> You have not because you ask not. (Jas 4:2)

The opposite is true, I asked, and God answered my prayers!

> This is the day the Lord has made; let us rejoice and be glad in it. (Ps 118:24)

I have included some pictures of Kipper and me!

Next I want to introduce you to someone I met who liked to ride as much as I did!

I Remember the Moment When God Gave Me My Dream Horse, Kipper

Chapter 11

I Remember the Moment When I Met My Friend, Billy

Roy and I left San Diego so he could take a job in Portland, Oregon. We bought a dream farm fifteen miles from the closest town. It was a twenty acre farm, lots of pasture for the horses!

We were so excited to have a farm, we got cows, chickens, pigs, and I decided to plant a huge garden.

Roy tilled up a half acre, and I planted everything I could think to plant.

I planted seven rows of zucchini! We had so much food we had to buy some baby pigs to eat it all!!

There was a small cabin on the property, and Roy and I had fun fixing it up. We put in a sliding glass door, and Roy built a huge deck. We would sit out on the deck and have dinner. We had a fantastic view of Mt. Hood covered in snow.

I also made a fire pit in the back yard. It was fun to sit by the fire and watch the moon come up from behind Mt. Hood.

We could ride from the farm to a canyon called Clear Creek Canyon. The creek was big enough to find holes for swimming. It was fun to ride for hours and cool off in the creek!

After we had lived there awhile, some people told me about a neighbor who lived back in the woods in a small cabin. They said they saw him ride his horse along the road, and that he loved to ride. His name was Billy.

One day there was a loud knock on the door. When I opened it, there was a man with a long gray beard dressed in farm clothes.

"I hear you are a horse lover!!" he said in a gruff voice.

"Are you Billy?" I asked.

It was Billy. He came in and we started talking about horses.

"Do you want to go riding?" he asked.

"Sure!" I answered.

Billy was 75 years old, so I thought we would go on a short ride. I was wrong. We rode that day for eight hours! I could not believe it. I was exhausted, and so was Kipper! I was 28, and I usually rode for about three or four hours at the most.

I could not believe the energy that he had. He has been an inspiration to me since I met him. I did not know my grandparents, and I had never been around someone 75 who had so much energy! He gave me hope.

"I want to be like Billy; I want to have his energy and be as healthy as he is at his age!" I said to myself.

He amazed me even more when I went to visit him at his cabin!

He lived a mile off the main road on 130 acres! The only thing he had in his cabin was a wooden table, two wooden chairs, a single bed, a large black barrel that he used for a wood stove and for cooking, a small couch, and a piano.

He had no phone, no tv, no radio, no running water, no electricity, no bathroom, not even an outhouse! He walked to a spring to get his water.

I found out that he loved to play the piano, he loved to play the violin, and he loved to recite poetry. He lived alone, had never been married, and loved to read the Bible.

Before I met him he had played in a musical group that would play in churches and in detention centers.

He had one picture on the wall. It was the famous picture of an old man with a gray beard sitting at a table with an open Bible. Billy looked just like that picture, except Billy was rail thin.

On his farm he had cows, sheep, goats, and seventeen horses.

Sometimes I left Kipper and my other horse, Black, on his property to graze. It was fun to ride to a nearby pond to swim. There was a wooden raft on the pond for the kids to float around on.

I loved taking Kipper to the very end of his property and then running across open fields to his cabin! Even though Black did not have a rider, he ran alongside us!

One time when I was sitting in his cabin, Billy suddenly opened the door and called out, "Baby Doll! Here, Baby Doll!"

His pet goat came bounding into his cabin. He put a pan of grain down for her, and then he milked her while she ate! After he filled his cup, he added some chocolate syrup, stirred it around, and then drank it.

"Want some?" he asked.

"No thanks," I answered.

A moment to remember! It is so vivid it could have happened yesterday!

One day I went out to visit him so I could take his kittens to a pet store for him.

"I can't find the kittens!" he said in a frustrated voice.

A little later, he came back from the back of the cabin. He was carrying a fox pelt hat that I had made for him.

"I found them!"

All four kittens were curled up inside his hat!

Two other favorite memories come to my mind.

One time for Mother's day, Roy and I took the kids out to see him and have a picnic. We were sitting in the shade enjoying the day. Micki was gone for a while, and then she showed up with a big bouquet of wild flowers for me!!

Another time, we decided to take the kids to Billy's for the fourth of July.

We sat around a little bonfire. The kids set off a few fire crackers, and then lit some sparklers. It was a special fourth of July because it was so simple. There we were in the middle of the woods, celebrating the fourth of July with Billy who served in World War I!

When he turned 90, I had a birthday party for him. I made a huge ice cream cake, and we put 90 candles on it!! He blew them all out!

During his party Billy played his violin with a friend who played the guitar, and he had the time of his life! He also recited his favorite poem.

I thought it was so amazing that he lived all alone in the middle of the woods, but he was a person who loved to perform!

I also thought it was amazing that he always seemed so happy!

I have never met anyone else in my whole life that had a twinkle in his eye the way that he did. He just loved living life!!

I would visit Billy often. Once I got there, we would walk outside and sit down on the ground under a huge cherry tree that was covered with pink blossoms. He did not even own any lawn chairs.

He loved telling me stories about his life. When he served in World War I, he took care of the horses. He told me he regretted not getting married or having children. I don't think there was any woman out there anywhere who could live the way that he did! He had the money to improve his cabin, but he loved the challenge of living a simple, simple life.

I thought Billy would live to be 100, but he died at 93. I know when I get to heaven he will meet me. He will be on his favorite big white horse, King, and he will have Kipper with him for me to ride!

He will say, "Are you ready to ride?" And I will say, "Sure!"

Now I would like to share his favorite poem with you:

> The Touch of the Master's Hand
> It was battered and scarred and the auctioneer
> Scarce thought it worth his while
> To spend much time with the old violin
> But he picked it up with a smile
> "What am I offered?" to folks he said;
> "Who will start the bidding for me?"
> "A dollar, a dollar, who'll make it two,
> Three dollars once, three dollars twice,"
> Going, going . . . but no!

Far back in the crowd an old gray-haired man
Came forward and picked up the bow
He wiped the dust from the old violin
Then he tightened the loosened strings
He played a melody pure and sweet
As a caroling angel sings
The music ceased and the auctioneer
In a voice that was quiet and low
Said, "Now what am I offered for the old violin?"
As he held it up with the bow
"One thousand, who'll make it two
Two thousand, who'll make it three
Three thousand once, three thousand twice,
Going, going . . . and gone!" cried he
The people cheered and some of them cried,
"We don't understand . . . what changed its worth?"
Quick came the reply,
"The touch of the Master's hand."
Many a man with his life out of tune
So deeply scarred with sin
Is auction cheap to the thoughtless crowd
Much like the old violin
A mess of pottage, a glass of wine,
A game and he travels on
Going once, going twice, going . . . and almost gone
But the Master comes and the foolish crowd
Never quite understands
The worth of a soul, and the change was wrought
By the touch of the Master's hand.

—Myra Brooks Welch

I have included some favorite pictures of Billy.

In the first picture, Billy is sitting in the grass. Next you will see him with his favorite cow in front of his cabin. Next you will see a picture of me singing his song to him for the first time, and then there is the picture of Micki, Mitch, Babydoll, and Billy. The last picture was taken when he played the violin at his birthday party. He was wearing the fox pelt hat I made him, and the rabbit pelt vest I made him.

I Remember the Moment When I Met My Friend, Billy

Amazing Moments to Remember

Chapter 12

I Remember the Moment When I Started a Fun Club

I learned something very important about myself when I was ten years old . . . *I like to have fun!*

I remember jumping rope on the sidewalk in front of my house, and I said to myself, "*I am having fun!*" And then I said to myself, "*I should help other people have fun, too.*"

I felt inspired and motivated to take action on my revelation about helping other people to have fun!

There was an empty room in my garage, and it looked like it would be the perfect place to have a club, a *fun club*!

I cleaned it up, found folding chairs, songbooks from somewhere, and then made a big sign for the front door. I wrote *fun club* in large letters in red and tacked it to the door.

Now I needed some members for the club!

I walked all over the neighborhood and invited everyone who was about my age to come to the first meeting of the *fun club*. I charged thirty-five cents to come! Once I got some money, I went to the store and spent it all on candy!

The date came, and kids showed up! We ate all the candy, and then I got the songbooks out.

When I looked at the songs, I realized two things: I did not know any of the songs, and I was a terrible singer! Everyone was looking at me. Now what was I going to do?

Suddenly, I got an idea. "Does anyone here know how to play football?" I asked. No one knew.

"Let's go to the football field and play football," I said, "It will be fun!"

I ran upstairs and got my brother's football, and then led them one block away to the high school football stadium.

I divided everyone into two teams. I got to be a quarterback because I knew how to throw a spiral pass.

We played football for about an hour, and I thought it was fun! I don't know if anyone else did.

That was my one *fun club* meeting! I do not remember ever meeting again, but I actually had fun for one meeting!

It is all so vivid to me, and it showed me something very important about my personality that has lasted a lifetime. *I like to have fun, and help other people to have fun, too!*

This story helps explain the miracle that God did for me later in my life so that I could have fun, and help other people to have fun, too!

Here is one of my favorite scriptures:

> I am with you and will watch over you wherever you go.
> (Gen 28:15)

Now I will explain this *amazing miracle.*

Chapter 13

I Remember the Moment When I Became Banjo Beth

Do you remember the scripture I quoted earlier?

> All glory to God, who is able through His mighty power at work within us, to accomplish infinitely *more than we can ask or think*. (Eph 3:20)

To me, that is what I call a *miracle*. It is a miracle when God does something in my life that I did not ask Him to do, and something that I had never even thought about doing!

That is why I call this story a *miracle*!!

It all started one day when I was sitting by a creek basking in the sun. All of a sudden, I heard a song. I heard the words and the melody. I heard three different verses and the chorus. It was very clear, and I started singing it over and over again. The name of the song was "Take Them into the Land of Milk and Honey."

This was shocking to me because I am not a good singer. I could not remember any song except "Happy Birthday" and "Jesus Loves Me."

The song did not go away, I kept hearing it, and so I kept singing it.

Why did God give me this song? I went home, and wrote down the words so I would not forget them.

That was just the beginning!!
I started hearing one song after another!!!
I kept writing down the words, and hoped I would remember the melody. What in the world was happening?

I wrote a song about Micki, about Mitch, about Billy, about Roy, and one about me called "Banjo Beth"!!

After I wrote the song "Banjo Beth," I bought a banjo!!

I wrote a song called "When I Get to Heaven," and a song called "Listen to the Voice of the Lord."

Then one day I wrote the song "Holy Spirit Hoedown" . . . and a song called "Let's Celebrate Today!!"

Once I had written fifteen songs, I decided to see if they could be recorded. I called and talked to Scott Hybl who had just opened his own recording studio. I explained to him what had happened.

"Sing all the songs onto a tape and bring it to me so I can hear them," he said.

Then I waited to hear from him. Finally, he called.

"*I think these songs would make a great tape for children,*" he said.

I decided to record the songs!! It took one year to produce the tape. I asked friends of mine to sing the songs. I was on five of the songs. Scott wrote the background music for each song.

It was a thrill to be in a recording studio! It was a thrill to hear each song come to life with singers and music!!

All year I prayed and asked God what he wanted me to do with the songs.

One day, *God gave me a vision!*

I saw myself going into churches and into Christian schools to share the songs!! I saw myself singing up on stage and putting on a country hoedown for the whole family!

The songs were very electric and fun to sing!! What was the purpose of the songs?

Just like my fun club . . . I felt my job was to have fun, and help other people have fun too!!

As soon as the songs were released, I started sharing the songs in schools and in churches for the entire family. There are several special events I would like to tell you about.

A friend of mine invited me to come to Seattle to put on a Country Hoedown for her church. Everyone wore western clothes and cowboy hats. There were about 200 people there. It started with a pot luck dinner, followed by a square dance for the whole family.

Next it was time to share the songs. I had several other people sing songs and perform, too. One of those people was Billy. He was ninety years old at that time.

He wore a beautiful new white cowboy shirt with a large red rose on each shoulder. There was a spotlight on him. He recited his favorite poem, and then he played the violin. You could have heard a pin drop. People were in awe of him. It was the best performance of his life. He played "Amazing Grace" on the violin, and everyone sang along. A moment I will never forget.

Another event I will never forget is the one where I went into a large Christian school. All ages attended, from kindergarten through seniors in high school. First they had a chili feed for lunch, and then I started sharing my songs.

It was fun because the students joined me and performed songs, too. What I really loved was when I sang the song "Holy Spirit Hoedown"; the kids jumped up on the stage with me and danced all the way through the song!!

It made me feel so good, because I was having fun, and I was helping other people to have fun, too!!

Another favorite memory for me was when I went into the local detention center. I was so happy to see how much the kids there enjoyed the songs!

I performed the songs for five years, and then it was time to just share the tape of songs.

One parent said, "My kids will not stop listening to it, and now they have memorized every song on the tape!"

My pastor told me that when he was driving in the car, he asked his kids if they wanted to listen to Michael Jackson, or Banjo Beth. They said, "Banjo Beth"!

Somehow I believe the Banjo Beth songs will go worldwide, or maybe be a Broadway musical!!

I love these songs!!

I have talked to adults who listened to the songs as children, and now they play it for their children!

You have to agree, God did a *huge miracle* when He gave me the Banjo Beth songs.

I hope someday you can actually hear them!

It has always been fun for me to watch the reaction of children when they hear the songs! They usually start singing along, and start dancing around the room!

One day Mitch gave me a huge compliment.

"You need to be on TV so kids can hear your Banjo Beth songs," he said.

Here is a favorite scripture:

> I have come that they may have life, and have it to the full. (John 10:10)

I have included a picture of "Banjo Beth"!

Now it is time for me to tell you about *another huge miracle* He did in my life!

I Remember the Moment When I Became Banjo Beth

Chapter 14

I Remember the Moment When God Gave Me Winnervision

WHAT IS WINNERVISION? THAT is the name of the seminar I have been teaching to students and athletes for the past 40 years.

The purpose of *Winnervision* is to help athletes stay focused under pressure. It will help them stay relaxed, cool, calm and re-laxed under pressure.

I would like to share a true story with you about one of my tennis players. It will help you understand what *Winnervision* is all about in just one story.

I was coaching tennis at the University of California at San Diego. I went to watch Kate play her match. She was our number one singles player.

She lost her match badly; I had never seen her play like that before.

"Kate, what were you thinking about while you were playing your match?"

"I was thinking about what I did wrong on my chemistry test," she replied.

So there you have it. She showed up physically, but mentally she was still at her chemistry test. *She was not there.*

After coaching four years, I found that most players were mentally focused about 50% of the time. As a player I experienced the same problem, so I was not able to help them stay focused. I needed to learn how to stay focused so I could help them.

I prayed for God's help. He led me to people to talk to, and books to read so that I could learn how to stay focused.

It happened! I learned to stay focused!

I learned how to stay relaxed, cool, calm and collected under pressure. Instead of being focused 50% of the time, I was able to stay focused 90% of the time!

What did I learn that helped me to stay focused?

First, *I learned to stop dwelling on my mistakes*, and see my mistakes as *temporary setbacks*. I learned to *let go* of my mistakes *so I could stay in present time*.

I learned to visualize the performance I wanted, and mentally prepare for pressure situations at the end of the game. This is what helped me stay relaxed when the pressure was on.

I learned to stop putting myself down and I learned to change my self-talk from negative to positive. I learned to tell myself "I have unlimited potential."

Once I had all this information together, I prayed for a way to share it. I did not know how to get started. God answered my prayers.

I was visiting friends in San Diego, and I was on the campus at the University of California at San Diego, when I ran into a friend I had worked with for years. His name was Bob Moss.

He invited me to attend a seminar he taught to motivate students. After the seminar, he asked me to come to his office the next day because he wanted to talk to me.

I went to his office and sat down. He had played football in the past, he was about 6'3," and about 350 pounds. He had a very strong presence.

"Why aren't you teaching motivational seminars? You are a motivator."

I was shocked by his question. No one had ever called me a *motivator* before.

"I have thought about it, but I don't know how to get started," I replied.

"First, you need to decide to do it, and then you will know how to get started," he explained.

"*I am not letting you leave my office until you say that you will do it,*" he added.

I was stunned. I thought about it for about thirty seconds, and then I said, "*Okay, I will do it.*"

"Great, thanks for coming in to see me," he said.

As soon as I left his office, *God gave me a vision!*

I saw myself teaching seminars to athletic teams, and students of all ages!! I saw athletes win state and national championships!

I started teaching seminars in my living room, and then I was invited to go into athletic clubs, and schools.

I saw dramatic results! My vision became reality!

I saw athletes win state and national championships!

I worked with athletes in every sport! I worked with students to help their grades improve so they could earn college scholarships.

Several months ago I made a *Winnervision* video and put it on YouTube. Type in. . . . "winnervision beth josi." It is all small letters. In the first twenty minutes I share how to stay focused, and then I share dramatic success stories. I made it as simple and as easy to understand as possible. It is only 40 minutes long.

I personally use *Winnervision* to help me stay focused every day. It helps me to see my mistakes as *temporary setbacks*. It helps me *let go* of negative experiences. It helps me focus on the positive things that I believe God wants me to do. I have learned to live in *present time*. I *visualize* accomplishing every goal that I have. I tell myself that I have "*unlimited potential*," and ask God to help me see myself being successful.

Peter is fourteen and Lydia is sixteen. They watched the video, and now they are both getting straight A's! Lydia has decided to become an attorney! I am hoping you will watch the video too!

Chapter 15

I Remember the Moment When God Gave Me a Heavenly Attic Bed and Breakfast

I FEEL LIKE I am living in heaven!! Sometimes I ask friends, "Did I die? Maybe I am really living in heaven!"

This story begins when my landlord called me and told me he was raising my rent $250 starting the next month. I tried to pay it for a few months, and then I decided to give notice, and try to find cheaper rent. The very day I decided to give notice, my friend Margie came to visit, so I told her I wanted to move even though I didn't know where to live. She loaned me some money to make it possible to move out.

Once I gave notice, I told my friend Linaya. She lives in Billings, Montana.

"I just gave one month's notice, and I have no idea where I am going to live," I said.

"Beth, I need you to come to Billings and take care of my cats for me," she replied.

I will be gone taking care of my mother, and it would really help me if you could come for three months and take care of my cats." It was settled. I decided to go to Billings at the end of the month.

It gave me one month to try to find a place to live after I left Billings. I had a housesitting job for the month of July, but did not know where I would live after that.

I went out to the farm where I leased a horse from a lady named Darcy.

"I am looking for a room to rent," I told her. "Do you still have a room for rent upstairs in your house?"

"Yes, I just offered it to a friend who is a contractor, but he turned it down. He said it was too far from his job," she explained.

"Could I see it?" I asked.

"OK," she replied.

We walked into her house through the kitchen to get to the stairs. Once I got upstairs, I was shocked. The room she rented was actually the entire upstairs of the house. It had a small second bedroom and a bathroom.

It was full of junk. It had been trashed by her last renter. All the walls were filthy, and there was smoke on the walls from a chimney fire.

As soon as I got to the top of the stairs and saw the size of the room, *God gave me a vision!*

I saw what the room would look like once I had a chance to clean everything out, and paint it. I knew it could be beautiful!!

"Could I clean it and paint it in trade for rent?" I asked.

"That would be fine with me. You can pick out the color of paint you want, and I will pay for the paint," she said.

It was decided. I could start in July when I got back from Billings.

I knew a friend who needed a place to stay, so she moved into my duplex and took care of my furniture, and my cat, GW.

Once I got to Billings, she lost phone service. I just had to pray GW was okay. She fed him outside and did not let him in the house.

I was in Billings for three months, and then when I came back to Oregon I started housesitting for a house about 45 minutes away from Darcy's. I was relieved to find out GW was okay, and I moved him into Darcy's.

Next I hired three high school boys to help clear out all the junk, and put what Darcy wanted to keep in storage.

I washed all the walls! Next, I painted the entire room and bathroom with a primer. I picked out a soft antique white paint, and bought extra high gloss white paint for the trim. Once I had the living room painted, Darcy had carpet installed.

I found some white wicker shelves for in front of one of the windows, and a matching set of drawers. I found a small refrigerator with a freezer for $8. I found them all at the local thrift store. I cleaned a tall cabinet and painted it with extra high gloss white paint, and used it for my dishes.

I bought narrow black tables and turned them into counter tops for the kitchen. I bought a hot plate to use to cook, and a microwave, and got a large crockpot.

I found new beautiful lace curtains for the windows. There was a large window at each end of the room. The window by my bed has a spectacular view of a huge tree and fields across the road.

I put up a divider in the bathroom, and used one end to do the dishes. There were windows in the bathroom with a great view of the field across the street. I put in a new bathroom cabinet and sink, and a new shower head. I also bought some plywood to cover three holes in the wall in the bathroom, and then I used an electric screw driver and tacked up some tiles hanging down from the ceiling.

Micki decided to give me her queen sized bed, and then I moved my double bed into the small room for a guest room!

I painted the stairs with a soft green high gloss paint so they are washable.

To decorate, I found beautiful green ivy plants at Goodwill that all look real.

A friend of mine came to visit, his name was Noe. When he got to the top of the stairs, he said, "*Beth!! This is Heaven!!*"

Noe was a twenty-year-old friend who had rented a room from me when I rented out a second room in my duplex. He was visiting from Texas, and asked if he could spend the night.

"I could move the cushions from your couch into the small bedroom," he said. That is what he did. He seemed very pleased with himself for thinking of it.

"*That is the best guest room in the whole world!*" he said.

So I named it the Heavenly Attic Bed and Breakfast. Now it even has a real bed that is comfortable! It is fun to have friends come and stay. I write each person's name on a plaque and hang the plaque on the wall.

About six months ago, I got an urgent call from my friend, Deanne. She has six children, and she was going through a hard time because of a divorce.

She has a fourteen-year-old son, Peter. She asked me if he could stay with me for one week because of some family problems. A week sounded like a long time, but I said yes.

Little did we know one week would become five months!

We had time to get to know each other. We enjoyed watching movies together, and eating popcorn. We watched some inspiring Christian movies.

Peter had read the entire Bible, and it was fun to talk about stories in the Bible. Peter had just recommitted his life to the Lord, and so I was able to share with him how much God had helped me in my life.

I was happy because Peter wanted to watch my *Winnervision* video, and then it was fun to talk to him about how *Winnervision* had helped me stay focused in my life, and how it had helped other people.

Peter was so helpful because I was weeding to get ready to plant flowers by the back door downstairs. He helped me weed and plant the flowers. Then he helped set up a timer to water the flowers with soaker hoses. He helped me plant a dogwood tree and set up a soaker hose to water it.

My daughter, Micki, was thrilled because he helped her transform her front yard, and he helped build a stone walkway. She had hired other people to help her, but she said Peter was the best worker.

I took Peter to the club where I work out, hoping to interest him in working out, too.

He got very enthused about working out, and decided to use the carport rafters for bars so he could do pull-ups!! He started going running out on the road; and he started doing sit ups in the living room several times a day!!

When I went riding, he walked on the trail in front of us. He used a big branch and cleared the berry vines out of the trail ahead of us.

Sharing with Peter how God had helped me in my life was very healing for me, and having someone to talk to was very healing for him!

Like I told Peter, renovating the heavenly attic reminds me of the way that God renovates our lives. First he gets rid of all the stuff in our lives that makes our lives a mess, then he washes us the way I washed the walls. Next he gets rid of all the stains in our lives the way that I used a primer to seal the walls. Then, like I used a satin finish that made the walls glow, he fills us with His spirit to make us glow, too. I told Peter the heavenly attic feels like living in a cocoon. Just like a caterpillar, we get to be healed and be transformed into a butterfly!! We get to feel free of our past just like a butterfly! *God helps us to put the past in the past, and live in the present!*

Now I also call the heavenly attic a "house of healing"!

Favorite scriptures:

> The thief comes only to steal, kill and destroy; I have come that they may have life, and have it to the full. (John 10:10)

> Do not conform any longer to the pattern of this world, but be transformed by the renewing of your mind. (Rom 12:2)

> Now may the Lord of peace himself give you peace at all times and in every way. (2 Thess 3:16)

> I tell you the truth, whatever you bind on earth will be bound in heaven, and whatever you loose on earth will be loosed in heaven. (Matt 18:18)

I shared with Peter how I bind every negative memory and every negative thought because I know Satan wants me to dwell on everything negative. Then I loose love, joy, and peace and ask God to fill me with His Spirit every day. I believe God wants us to be happy and healthy so we can be free to do everything that He wants us to do.

It was fun having Peter stay with me. Now he and his mother, Deanne, and his sixteen-year-old sister, Lydia, stay with me every other week-end. They live three hours away, but they drive to Molalla so that the four younger children can visit their father.

The four younger kids started asking if they could come to stay with me, too. Deanne and I decided it was time for a *family slumber party!*

The three youngest boys slept on the floor in sleeping bags, but they thought it was fun! They even brought their tiny dog, Sparkles! It is funny, because Sparkles is about one third the size of my cat!

I have included their family picture taken at the slumber party.

From left to right: Joseph, Caleb, Peter, Deanne, Lydia, Daniel, sitting in front of Deanne is Hanna and Sparkles!

We already have the next family slumber party planned for Christmas night!

Chapter 16

I Remember the Moment When I Became a Housesitter

I HAD BEEN CLEANING houses and doing organizing projects for people for five years, and wanted to find something else to do. I had been praying about it for over a year. Yes, God did another miracle, and answered my prayer!

One day I got a call from a friend who lived on the same street I did about five minutes away. Her name was Dorena.

"Beth, we are going to Hawaii with our boys, and need a housesitter. We need someone to feed our seven horses, and our dog. Could you housesit for us?"

"Sure, I would be happy to do it," I said.

"How much do you charge?" she asked.

"Charge? I thought I would do it for free," I said.

"No, housesitting is a job. You need to have a fee for each day that you are here," she explained.

"I don't know what to charge, just pay me whatever you want," I said.

Once they were in Hawaii, Dorena called me to see if everything was going OK.

"Is everything OK?" she asked.

"Could you stay longer? I think I want to become a housesitter," I said.

"*Good! I know people who need housesitters!!*" she answered.

That was the beginning of my Housesitting career!!

I had a sign made for my car that said, *housesitting, call Beth*, with my phone number. I also put up my housesitting card at all the feed stores.

The sign was on my car for one day, and I went into a little market. A lady came up to me and said, "Is that your car that says, housesitting?"

"Yes, it is," I replied.

"I am going to Australia for a month, and I need a housesitter," she said. That was one of the longest jobs I had ever had.

One time I was in a little restaurant, and a man came in the door and said,

"Who has a car out there that says, housesitting?"

"I do," I said.

His name was Arlyn, and I have become good friends with he and his wife Rita. They have two cute little dogs, Koco and Toby.

One time I was in a parking lot at a fabric store, and a lady said, "Do you have a card?" Her name was Karen.

One year later, she called me and asked me to housesit. I was shocked that she still had my card.

"I knew I would need a housesitter someday," she said.

Karen and I have become good friends. I took care of her black lab, Sam.

I bonded with Sam, and I was so fond of him I started taking him hiking and swimming at the Molalla river. I loved Sam!

When they no longer had Sam, they got a black lab puppy, Riley.

I took care of Riley for one weekend, and we totally bonded!

I love Riley! Now I take Riley hiking every Friday! He has so much fun because he can be off the leash! He can run all out! He can explore the trails, and go to the river to drink and swim.

We found a perfect swimming hole, and I decided to shock him and get in the water to swim with him! I got in the water first, and he couldn't believe I was in the water calling him!! It was so much fun to watch his reaction!

I Remember the Moment When I Became a Housesitter

He jumped as far out as he could, and then swam over to me! As soon as he got to me, I took his collar and turned him around me to swim back to shore. We did this over and over again!

Last Friday we drove to Cannon Beach so he could go running on the beach! I loved watching him chase the seagulls!!

One funny story happened when I was collecting eggs for a client named Eric. I was collecting the eggs in the barn, and one of the roosters attacked me from behind! I started yelling at him and kicking at him!! He would squawk and fly up in the air!! He thought it was a fun game!! The more I kicked at him, the more he liked it!!

One of my favorite jobs is with Buddy and Glenda Goodell. They have two Dachshunds, Zar and Zoey. It was funny because when I walked into the house to meet them, Zar and Zoey ran over to me and jumped into my lap!! It was like I was their best friend, but I had never met them before!!

"Our dogs love you, and so we love you, too!!" Glenda said.

I also think it is funny that the dogs come in to sleep with me when they do not sleep with Buddy or Glenda. So does the cat, Tiny. When I woke up last week-end, Zoey was under the cover being a perfect foot warmer, and Tiny was purring on my shoulder! It was impossible to get up! I was too comfortable!

It is also funny that their cat is bigger than the dogs, but his name is "Tiny"!

Once in a while I get to drive to the beach and take care of a Schnauzer, Fritz, and the cat, Sassy. It is fun to take Fritz walking every day in the salt air!

One day an amazing call came in. The people were looking for someone to take care of the chickens on their farm. They owned a farm with 100 acres, but they lived in Portland.

When I went out to the farm I was amazed at how beautiful it was. We agreed on a trade. I took care of the chickens in trade for pasture for my two horses. I got to ride on their property for three years!!

Years ago I took care of one of my favorite dogs named Baron. I am still in touch with his owner, Jan.

One day my friend, Linaya, said, "I think it is great that you came up with the idea to do housesitting. It is such a perfect job for you."

"*I cannot take any credit for the idea,*" I answered. "*I did not know housesitting was a job! God led me into it when I prayed for something new to do,*" I explained.

So God did it again!! He helped me find the perfect job!

> Before I formed you in the womb I knew you, before you were born I set you apart. (Jer 1:5)

> All glory to god, who is able through His mighty power at work within us, to accomplish infinitely more than we might ask or think. (Eph 3:20)

> I will instruct you and teach you in the way you should go; I will counsel you and watch over you. (Ps 32:8)

This is just one more example of how God answered my prayers. I wanted a new job, but *I had no idea* what that job could be!! I have been housesitting now for ten years, and hope to continue doing it forever!!

I have included a picture of Riley out on the trail! He is one happy dog!

Chapter 17

I Remember the Moment When I Became an Artist

ALL GLORY TO GOD, who is able through His mighty power at work within us, to accomplish infinitely *more than we can ask or think.* (Eph 3:20)

Here is another example when God gave me something I did not ask for or even think of doing!

This story begins when I was walking around at an art show. I came to some paintings that I really loved.

"Wow! I really love your style of painting!" I said to the artist.

"Maybe you would like to paint pictures, too," he said.

"No, I can't paint. I am not an artist," I replied.

"How do you know that you are not an artist? Have you ever tried to paint?" he asked.

"No, I have never tried to paint," I answered.

"I think you should try it. I think you would really enjoy it," he said.

God used him to convince me to try painting!

I took several lessons, and I painted a beautiful picture of our barn, the pasture, a big cherry tree, and our two horses grazing.

Friends asked me to paint pictures for them, too.

I did not have any more room on my wall for paintings!

God gave me an idea. Why not paint greeting cards?

Now I have painted over 100 greeting cards!

Painting is very relaxing, and just plain fun. It is a creative challenge. It is fun to try to see what I can paint. Sometimes I give up and throw it away. Sometimes I just keep trying. When it turns out, I absolutely love it!

Linaya has been my biggest inspiration. She loves my cards as much as I do, and she is always encouraging me to paint more cards!

Linaya has two of the most beautiful black cats I have ever seen. One has short hair, his name is Scamper. The other one has long hair, his name is Hopper.

Linaya asked me to paint a Christmas card for her. Now I do a Christmas scene with her two cats in the picture every year. This year both the cats are sitting in snow looking at a Christmas tree out in the woods. The Christmas star is in the sky.

She has a large family and so many friends, she just ordered 150 cards!

I became inspired to paint Christmas cards for my clients with their dogs or cats in the picture. It is a fun thank you gift that I can leave for them when they get back from vacation.

My client, Eric, had a dog that I loved named, Bjorn. He was a giant black Schnauzer. When I watched tv, I put my legs on the leg rest. Bjorn would climb up on the leg rest, stretch out on top of me, and put his head on my shoulder! He covered my entire body! He wanted to be a lap dog !

I was so upset when Eric called to tell me Bjorn had been hit by a car.

I was able to paint three cards for Eric. One was Bjorn's profile; one was of him running free in heaven; one was of him running on the beach.

I have included the profile of Bjorn so you can see it.

Even though I did not think I could ever be an artist, God made what seemed impossible, possible! I feel all my paintings are inspired by Him!

I Remember the Moment When I Became an Artist

Chapter 18

I Remember the Moment When I Became a Single Mother

I HAVE SOME FRIENDS who say they have been happily married for 50 years. I am not able to say that.

I have been a single mother now for 25 years. I prayed for years that Roy and I could be friends again like we once were.

I consider it a miracle, but finally we met several times to talk about our marriage. We both said we were sorry for whatever we did wrong in the marriage, and we forgave each other.

His wife, Nancy, befriended me. Now Roy and Nancy, Micki, Kristian, Mitch and I can all get together for holidays and birthdays. What a relief. It is so nice to all be able to enjoy being together.

Once a month Roy, Micki, Kristian, and Mitch get together for lunch and to play cribbage. It makes me feel so good to know they can be together and enjoy each other. So nice to put the past in the past, and live in the present.

The Lord has provided for me in so many ways through the years. Here are a few examples I would like to share with you.

One time I was driving on totally bald tires, hoping to buy some used tires in a month or so. Then I got a letter in the mail from Les Schwab.

I Remember the Moment When I Became a Single Mother

The letter told me I had a gift for $400 to get new tires! I was shocked!! Who would do that? The letter was signed, *Anonymous!!* I never found out who gave me that gift!!

One time I was praying about being broke. I went to the car, and there were two twenty dollar bills sitting on the front seat of my car!!

Another time I looked at my bank account, and I realized I was going to be overdrawn the next day.

I called a good friend because I was desperate.

"I have never asked you for a loan before, but I am going to be overdrawn at the bank in the morning," I explained. "Do you think I could borrow a couple hundred dollars?"

"I just sold my cabin at the beach, and I was planning on giving you one thousand dollars. What is your account number? I will put the money in right now," she answered.

One time I had left a job in Corvallis and I had plans to move to Molalla. I had $50 to my name. I was sitting at a table in a house that I had put a deposit on so that I could move there . . . somehow. I had plans to start cleaning houses, but I did not have any housecleaning jobs yet.

Roy just happened to come over that day to talk. When he left there was an envelope sitting on the table. I had not asked him for any money.

"That is for you," he said when he walked out the door.

I opened the envelope, and it was a check for $2,000.

It gave me the money to move, and time to start a business cleaning and organizing houses!

God did a miracle because I was able to start a full time business by putting one ad in the paper !

The ad said: *Excellent Housecleaning and Organizing, call Beth.*

All I know to do is to tithe at the first of the month, and then I pray that God will provide what I need to get through each month. In the Bible it says:

> "Bring the whole tithe into the storehouse, that there may be food in my house. Test me in this," says the Lord Almighty, "and see if I will not throw open the floodgates

of heaven and pour out so much blessing that you will not have room enough for it." (Mal 3:8–12)

Then Jesus said to his disciples: "Therefore I tell you, do not worry about your life, what you will eat; or about your body, what you will wear. Life is more than food, and the body more than clothes. Consider the ravens: they do not sow or reap, they have no storeroom or barn; yet God feeds them. And how much more valuable you are than the birds! Who of you by worrying can add a single hour to his life? Since you cannot do this very little thing, why do you worry about the rest?" (Luke 12:22–31)

You did not choose me, but I chose you and appointed you to go and bear fruit, fruit that will last. Then the Father will give you whatever you ask in my name. (John 15:16)

Every time I pray I ask for it in His name!

You are my servant; I have chosen you and not rejected you. So do not fear, for I am with you; do not be dismayed, for I am your God. I will strengthen you and help you; I will upheld you with my righteous hand. (Isa 41:9)

Faith is being sure of what we hope for and certain of what we do not see. (Heb 11:1)

I think about these scriptures, and try not to worry about how He is going to provide. *I choose to believe that He will provide . . . somehow.*

Chapter 19

I Remember the Moment When I Fell Apart

I HAD HEARD THE term "falling apart," but I had never experienced it. Why did I fall apart?

I had just finished remodeling a house, and needed to find a new job. I could not imagine what job I could find that I would want to do. All I could think about is how much I did not want to do every job that I thought about.

Gripped with fear for the first time in my life, I felt overwhelmed with depression.

I had a friend at that time who was going through a divorce, and she was totally depressed, too. We both talked about dying because it sounded like a way out of our depression. We were both suicidal.

One day, out of desperation, we decided to sit down together and forgive every person in our entire lives.

We each had a list of people to forgive, including ourselves. We both felt better afterwards; at least we had taken action in a positive way. Our depression seemed a little better.

I was still gripped with fear. I was going to see two counselors a week, just hoping I would feel better.

This went on for months. Then one day, while I was driving down the road, I began shouting out loud:

"I bind a spirit of fear in the name of the Father, the Son, and the Holy Spirit!! I release a spirit of peace and joy and love!!!"

The next day I was driving to see the counselor, suddenly, I saw a fog lift in front of me . . . *but it was not a foggy day!*

Suddenly, I felt overwhelmed with a spirit of peace. It was like a blanket of peace came over me, a peace that passes all understanding. I knew it was a peace that would stay with me. I knew that God was with me, and that he would provide for me.

When I got to the counselor, I said, " I will not be coming back. I feel fine, now. I know everything will work out."

"What? Do you have a job?" she asked.

"No, not yet. But that is okay. I will get a job when the time is right. I don't feel suicidal anymore; I am just unemployed."

Done. My depression was gone!! My fear was gone!! I knew God was with me, and that he would provide a job for me when the time was right!!!

That happened over twenty years ago, and the depression and fear never came back!!

I kept applying for jobs, but did not get a job for several months. I was unemployed for a total of six months. I had been living on my savings.

And then it happened! I was driving down the street when I saw a sign on a building about one mile from my house. The sign said: "Now Opening."

The building was Nelson's Nautilus Athletic Club. I went in and met one of the people who was in charge. He showed me around the club, and then he said, "Would you like to join?"

"Actually, I am looking for a job," I said.

I gave him my resume, and a booklet I had written explaining how I had worked with athletes teaching them to stay focused under pressure. Several of them had won state and national championships.

I got the job!! I was hired to work as a personal trainer, and to teach water aerobics. I worked at Nelson's Nautilus for six years!!

I loved working there because I became friends with the staff, and made many new friends that came into the club. Also, the staff encouraged me to teach *Winnervision* seminars. I taught the seminar every month for all ages. Every seminar averaged about 30 people.

The whole six months I was unemployed, they were building the club!

That is called . . . God's perfect timing!

I am actually glad that I fell apart. I learned compassion for other people who are falling apart. I can tell them I understand, because I have fallen apart, too.

Here are some favorite scriptures that helped me through my "falling apart" experience.

> I tell you the truth, whatever you bind on earth will be bound in heaven, and whatever you loose on earth will be loosed in heaven. (Matt 18:18)

> God does not give us a spirit of fear, but of love and power, and sound mind. (2 Tim 1:7)

> "For I know the plans I have for you" says the Lord. "They are plans for good and not for evil, to give you a future and a hope." (Jer 29:11)

Chapter 20

I Remember the Moment When I Read the Story of David and Goliath

I HAD HEARD THE story of David and Goliath, but I had never read the story in the Bible. The story about a young boy defeating a giant seemed so unreal. It was hard to believe that it was really a true story. And then I read it, and I realized it actually really happened. The story is also in the Encyclopedia.

The story about David and Goliath hit me so hard, I still think about it all the time. I would like to share with you why the story has helped me so much.

David was known as *a man after God's own heart*. Why?

The reason is because of the personal relationship he had with God. He talked to him; he sang praises to Him; he was totally honest with God about the way that he felt. He trusted God to be with him. He trusted God to help him and protect him.

David set a perfect example for me. If David could be that open and honest with God, then I should be that open and honest with God. It helped me to trust God to help me and protect me. God wants to have a personal relationship with us.

It was interesting to me that David spent years alone in the wilderness taking care of his father's sheep. That was a very important time in his life. He took his job seriously. He protected the sheep.

He felt God helped him protect the sheep when he was able to kill a bear and a lion. The bear and the lion could have killed not only the sheep, but him.

David spent hours sitting around the bon fire at night singing praises to God. He played a small hand harp, and wrote hundreds of songs to praise God that are found in the Psalms.

I can imagine going to visit him the way that I used to go out in the woods to visit Billy. I can imagine sitting on a stump by the fire listening to him sing and play his hand harp. I can imagine him having the most beautiful voice in the world. A voice like the Italian singer, Andre Bocelli. I can imagine the sky full of stars the way it is when you are in the wilderness.

During the day David had time to practice using his slingshot. His slingshot had a long leather strap. He would swing it around his head, and then release a stone at the right time. Warriors who were good at using slingshots were known as "slingers." David became an expert with his slingshot.

While David was out in the wilderness taking care of the sheep, the King of Israel was having problems. His name was Saul. He would hear from God, but he would not do what God asked him to do.

Samuel was the prophet of the day. He had spent time with Saul to try to help him do what God asked him to do, but finally God told Samuel that he rejected Saul as King.

Samuel was grieving the loss of Saul as King because he had invested so much time in him.

"How long are you going to grieve for Saul?" God asked.

"Take your horn of oil and go to the house of Jesse. I will anoint one of Jesse's sons as the new King."

Samuel went to the house of Jesse, and asked to meet all his eight sons.

Once he got there he was impressed with their appearance. They were tall and strong.

"I do not look at the outward appearance, I look at the heart," God said.

Samuel started to anoint the oldest son, but God said, "*No, he is not the one.*"

This happened every time he started to anoint one of the sons. Now there was no one left. Samuel was puzzled.

"Do you have another son?" he asked Jesse.

"Yes, my youngest son, David. He is out taking care of my sheep."

"Bring him in," Samuel said.

Once David walked in, God told Samuel, "*He is the one.*"

So Samuel poured the oil over David and anointed him as the new king.

David went back to take care of the sheep because he was only seventeen years old. He did not actually become king for twenty years.

Saul was overwhelmed with depression because of evil spirits that would visit him. He asked to have a minstrel come to sing to him to calm him down.

One of his servants said, " I know of a young man who sings with a hand harp, and the Lord is with him,"

"Bring him to me," Saul said.

You guessed it. He was talking about David. So David was asked to visit Saul and play the harp and sing for him. It helped to calm Saul down. Then he would return to take care of his father's sheep.

One day Jesse asked David to take a donkey with some food to check on his three oldest brothers, who were in the army for Israel.

David arrived at the battle field and gave the food to his brothers.

All of a sudden, a huge giant stood up on a hill across a valley and starting shouting to the warriors of Israel.

"Send a man to fight me! If I win, you will be our slaves! If he wins, we will be your slaves!" he shouted.

All the warriors for Israel were afraid to fight Goliath. He was over nine feet tall, covered with bronze armor. He had been shouting the same thing every morning and every night for 40 days.

I Remember the Moment When I Read the Story of David and Goliath

Saul had offered a reward to anyone who would go out to fight Goliath. He offered his daughter in marriage, and to be exempt from paying taxes. But no one cared about the reward. They knew to fight Goliath meant death. *It was an impossible situation.*

David stood on a hill across the valley and listened to him shouting to them.

I believe that at that moment, God gave David a vision.

David saw himself bringing Goliath down with his slingshot, and then using Goliath's sword to cut off his head.

He asked to talk with Saul. Saul was shocked to see him.

"David! What are you doing here?" He remembered David because David sang to him to calm him down. " Are you here to sing to me?"

"*I want to fight Goliath*," David said.

"What? Fight Goliath? That is impossible! You cannot fight Goliath! Goliath is nine feet tall, covered in armor, and a champion in his army! He has been in the army as long as you have been alive! He has a sword, a spear, and a javelin. You are seventeen years old, a shepherd, and a singer. What makes you think that you can fight Goliath?"

"I have been watching and listening to Goliath. *God gave me a vision. I can see myself bringing Goliath down with my slingshot, and then cutting off his head*," David said.

"But what if you lose? Then our entire army loses," Saul said.

"Don't worry. I am not going out there to lose. God will be with me. When I was taking care of my father's sheep, God helped me to kill a bear and a lion. They could have killed me and the sheep. *God has prepared me for this battle.* I practice every day with my slingshot. I always hit my target. I never miss. When I defeat Goliath, the whole world will know that there is a living God in Israel!" David answered.

"You will need some armor, and I have armor that you could wear," Saul said.

David tried it on but it did not fit him; it was too big.

"I cannot wear this armor. It does not fit, and it would slow me down. I am going to run straight at Goliath. I need to be able to move around quickly. I might need to dodge his spear. You will see me bring him down with my slingshot, and cut off his head, " David said.

"How are you going to cut off his head?" Saul asked. " You are going out there without a sword."

"*I will use his*," David answered.

Finally, Saul agreed to let him go.

"*May God be with you*," Saul said.

On the way to meet Goliath, David stopped at a stream at the bottom of the valley and picked up five smooth stones to put in his bag.

David went out to meet Goliath. When Goliath saw him, he became furious.

"*I will kill you and feed you to the birds of the air!*" he screamed.

> David said to the Philistine, "You come against me with a sword and spear and javelin, but I come against you in the name of the Lord Almighty, the God of the armies of Israel, whom you have defied.
>
> This day the Lord will hand you over to me, and I'll strike you down and cut off your head. Today I will give the carcasses of the Philistine army to the birds of the air and the world will know that there is a God in Israel.
>
> All those gathered here will know that it is not by sword or spear that the Lord saves; for the battle is the Lord's and He will give all of you into our hands."
>
> As the Philistine moved closer to attack him, David ran quickly toward the battle line to meet him.
>
> Reaching into his bag and taking out a stone, he slung it and struck the Philistine on the forehead. The stone sank into his forehead, and he fell face down on the ground.
>
> So David triumphed over the Philistine with a sling and a stone; without a sword in his hand he struck down the Philistine and killed him. Then he drew Goliath's sword, and cut off his head. (1 Sam 17:45–50).

I Remember the Moment When I Read the Story of David and Goliath

So I have been inspired because God was with David, and gave him the victory. *It is the most famous battle in history, because God helped David do the impossible.*

I marvel over how God prepared David, and gave him a vision to do the impossible. That is why I think about the story of David and Goliath so often.

God has given me visions, and helped me to do what seemed impossible for me, too.

A friend of mine went to Israel and brought me a rock from the stream where David fought Goliath. I have it sitting in glass on my desk as a *constant* reminder about David's victory over Goliath.

> No eye has seen nor ear has heard what God has prepared for those who love Him. (1 Cor 2:9)

> Faith is being sure of what we hope for and certain of what we do not see. (Heb 11:1)

Chapter 21

I Remember the Moment When I Read the Story of Joshua and Caleb

THE STORY OF JOSHUA and Caleb hit me really hard just like the story of David and Goliath.

> The Lord said to Moses, "Send some men to explore the land of Canaan, which I am giving to the Israelites. From each ancestral tribe send one of its leaders." (Num 13:1–3)

> When the spies searched the Valley of Eshcal, they cut off a branch bearing a single cluster of grapes. Two of them carried it on a pole between them, along with some pomegranates and figs. (Num 13:23)

> At the end of forty days they returned from exploring the land. (Num 13:25)

> They gave Moses this account: "We went into the land to which you sent us, and it does flow with milk and honey! Here is the fruit. But the people who live there are powerful and the cities are fortified and very large." . . . Then Caleb silenced the people before Moses and said, "*We should go up and take possession of the land, for we can certainly do it.*"

I Remember the Moment When I Read the Story of Joshua and Caleb

But the men who had gone up with him said, *"We can't attack those people, they are larger than we are."*

And they spread among the Israelites a bad report about the land they had explored.

They said, *"The land we explored devours those living in it. All the people we saw there are of great size. We seemed like grasshoppers in our own eyes, and we looked the same to them!"* (Num 13:26-28, 30-33)

So the men Moses had sent to explore the land, who returned and made a whole community grumble against him by spreading a bad report about it . . . *these men responsible for spreading the bad report about the land were struck down and died of a plague before the Lord.*

Of the men who went to explore the land, only Joshua and Caleb survived. (Numbers 14:36-38)

Now do you see why the story of Joshua and Caleb hit me so hard? It is a very strong message . . . if God asks you to do something, even if it seems impossible . . . He wants us to believe He will be with us and help us accomplish it!!!

In Closing

When I was talking to my friend Linaya about this book, I told her what had happened when we were eighteen years old.

"When I was visiting your house when we were eighteen, I was sitting on the back porch with your mother. I told your mother, "Someday, I am going to write a book."

"Really? What will it be about?" she asked.

"It will be a book about the experiences from my life," I explained.

I had totally forgotten that I ever said that. It just came back to me recently.

Four years ago, I wrote five stories about my life. Linaya and her mother read them together, and it sparked a conversation about their own relationship with God. They had never talked about their faith before. From that conversation, Linaya wrote a devotion every day to share with her mother.

She has thanked me for writing those stories over and over again. Her mother passed away two years ago, but at least I got to share five stories with her.

When Linaya and I were eighteen, I shared an important scripture with her.

> I am certain that God who began the good work within you, will continue His work until it is finally finished on the day when Christ Jesus returns. (Phil 1:6)

Here are some important scriptures I would like to share with you in case you are interested in becoming a Christian.

In Closing

For God so loved the world that He sent His one and only son so whosoever believes in Him will have eternal life. (John 3:16)

Here I am! Behold, I stand at the door and knock! Any man that hears my voice and opens the door, I will come in and eat with him, and he with me. (Rev 3:20)

That is Jesus speaking, asking to come into your heart. He cannot come into your heart unless you open the door and invite him in. Once you ask Jesus into your heart, then you are promised eternal life. God's spirit is then with you to lead you and protect you and help you find God's will for your life.

There are so many scriptures I would like to share with you, but I think it is amazing that God tells us *"Fear not, I am with you"* 365 times!!

What I have wanted to do is to inspire and encourage you because God has helped me so much. Why? Because I have asked for His help, and then when He told me what to do, I did my best to do it. I am still amazed that it is possible to hear God's voice. We can talk to Him like we talk to each other.

I asked Him to come into my life, and fill me with His spirit. I have asked Him to forgive my sins, and fill me with love, joy, and peace. He has helped me to learn how to live in present time. I have learned to put the past in the past, which gives me peace of mind. I have asked Him to show me the way. I constantly ask Him what He wants to do with my life.

Can God really know us, and forgive us, and fill us with His spirit? It seems too good to be true, I know.

Where I went wrong for a while is when I tried to earn His love, and I burned out. He does not want us to earn it. He just wants to give His love. It is called the grace of God. We can never do enough to earn it.

So of course, I would love to hear from you!

I am saying the same thing to you that Saul said to David: *"May God be with you!"*

Beth Josi
P.O. Box 1309
Molalla, Oregon
bethjosi@hotmail.com
(503) 984-3244

www.ingramcontent.com/pod-product-compliance
Lightning Source LLC
Chambersburg PA
CBHW071159090426
42736CB00012B/2381